Color Me UNDER THE SEA

An Adorable Coloring Book

Illustrations by Shyaoman Zhang

CIDER MILL PRESS

BOOK PUBLISHERS

Introduction

If you're reading this, you're our kind of person. Maybe you're stressed out from work or exhausted by your social life—or maybe you're totally zen already and just looking for a creative outlet (tell us your secrets, please). For whatever reason, you've decided to unwind with this adorable coloring book. You've chosen the right activity; coloring books are proven to reduce anxiety and lift negative moods.

These delightful designs are suitable for all skill levels. The pages are one-sided, so your art won't bleed through. You can use whatever tool you want to fill in these charming illustrations: colored pencils, markers, gel pens, watercolors, crayons, you name it. Color inside the lines or outside of them—the point is to relax and create something that makes you happy.

These detailed illustrations allow you to practice mindfulness and will keep you busy for hours. You can enjoy the meditative benefits in silence, or maybe you'd like to curate a different kind of calming atmosphere with some music. You can even invite a friend to color with you; this book makes a great gift.

However you choose to bring these cute marine creatures to life, we're sure that you'll enjoy unleashing your inner artist with these beautiful illustrations. Share your enchanting creations with the world by posting on social media with the hashtag #colormeunderthesea (and be sure to tag us @cidermillpress)! Now go forth and find your bliss with *Color Me Under the Sea.*

The world can be an ugly place.
Brighten it up with these adorable animals!
Life got you stressed out? Take some time
for yourself. Focus on the journey, not the
destination, as you explore the intricate detail
of these stunning illustrations. The destination
will be satisfying no matter how you get there!
Frame your masterpieces to beautify your
own space, or bring joy to someone else by
gifting them your charming creations.
Now open up to any page—it's time
to add some color to your day!

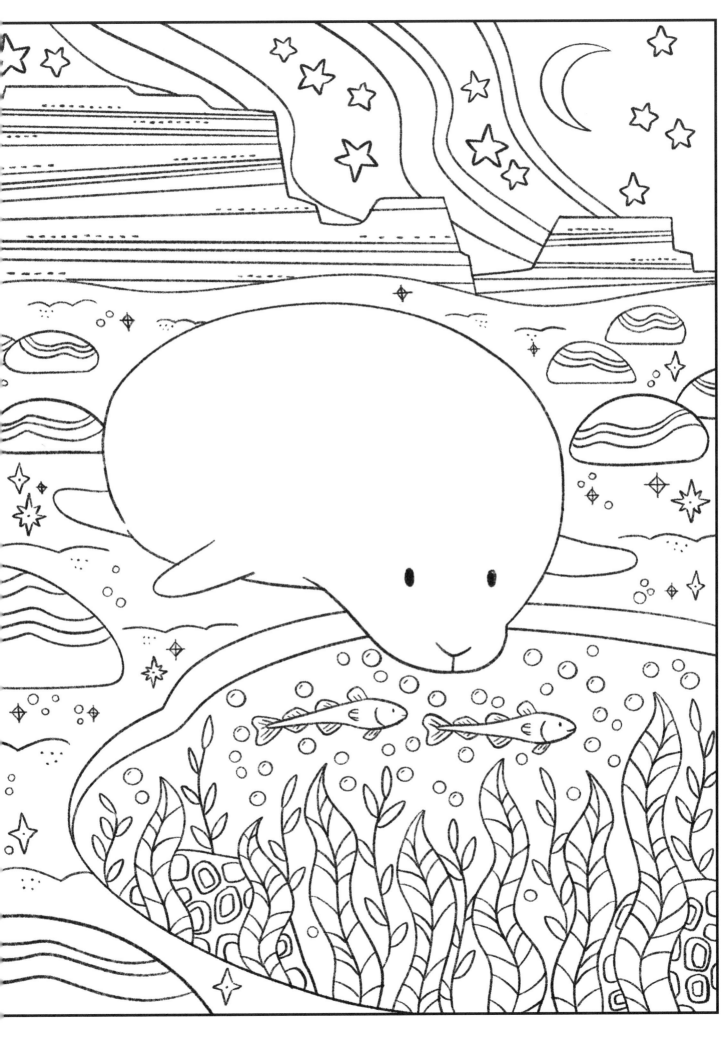

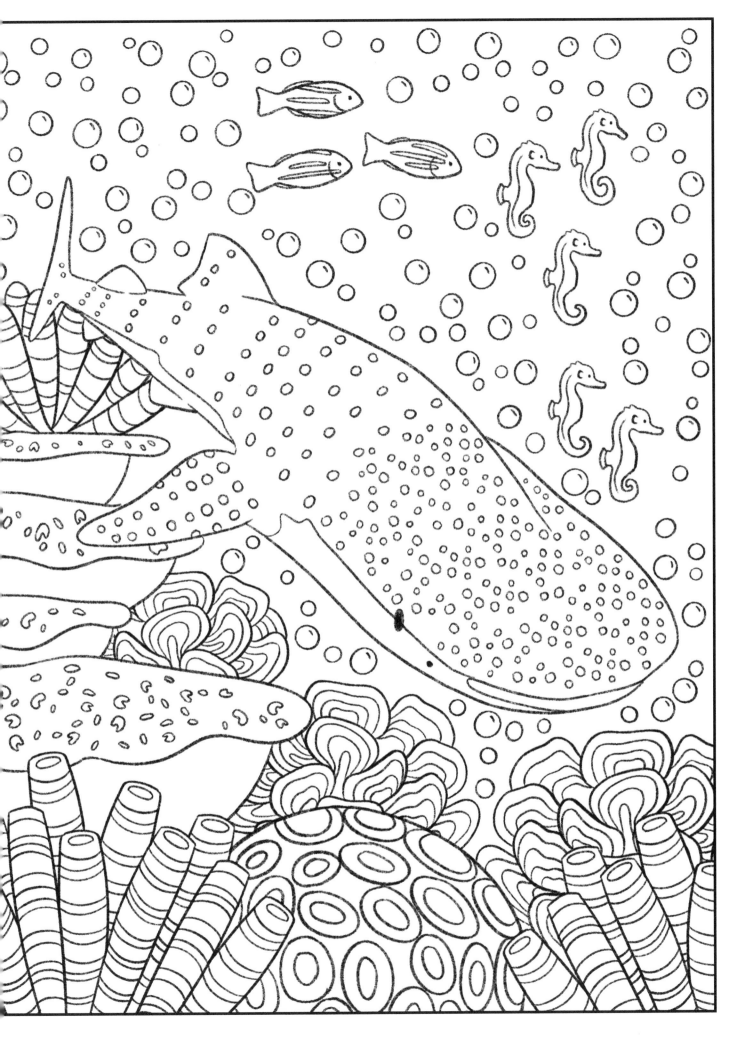

Share Your
MASTERPIECES

Don't keep your colorful creations
to yourself—take a pic and share it
on social media with the hashtag
#colormeunderthesea and
tag us @cidermillpress!

#COLORMEUNDERTHESEA #COLORMEUNDERTHESEA
#COLORMEUNDERTHESEA #COLORMEUNDERTHESEA
#COLORMEUNDERTHESEA #COLORMEUNDERTHESEA
#COLORMEUNDERTHESEA #COLORMEUNDERTHESEA
#COLORMEUNDERTHESEA #COLORMEUNDERTHESEA
#COLORMEUNDERTHESEA #COLORMEUNDERTHESEA
#COLORMEUNDERTHESEA #COLORMEUNDERTHESEA
#COLORMEUNDERTHESEA #COLORMEUNDERTHESEA
#COLORMEUNDERTHESEA #COLORMEUNDERTHESEA
#COLORMEUNDERTHESEA #COLORMEUNDERTHESEA
#COLORMEUNDERTHESEA #COLORMEUNDERTHESEA
#COLORMEUNDERTHESEA #COLORMEUNDERTHESEA
#COLORMEUNDERTHESEA #COLORMEUNDERTHESEA
#COLORMEUNDERTHESEA #COLORMEUNDERTHESEA
#COLORMEUNDERTHESEA #COLORMEUNDERTHESEA
#COLORMEUNDERTHESEA #COLORMEUNDERTHESEA
#COLORMEUNDERTHESEA #COLORMEUNDERTHESEA
#COLORMEUNDERTHESEA #COLORMEUNDERTHESEA
#COLORMEUNDERTHESEA #COLORMEUNDERTHESEA
#COLORMEUNDERTHESEA #COLORMEUNDERTHESEA
#COLORMEUNDERTHESEA #COLORMEUNDERTHESEA
#COLORMEUNDERTHESEA #COLORMEUNDERTHESEA
#COLORMEUNDERTHESEA #COLORMEUNDERTHESEA
#COLORMEUNDERTHESEA #COLORMEUNDERTHESEA

#COLORMEUNDERTHESEA #COLORMEUNDERTHESEA
#COLORMEUNDERTHESEA #COLORMEUNDERTHESEA
#COLORMEUNDERTHESEA #COLORMEUNDERTHESEA
#COLORMEUNDERTHESEA #COLORMEUNDERTHESEA
#COLORMEUNDERTHESEA #COLORMEUNDERTHESEA
#COLORMEUNDERTHESEA #COLORMEUNDERTHESEA
#COLORMEUNDERTHESEA #COLORMEUNDERTHESEA
#COLORMEUNDERTHESEA #COLORMEUNDERTHESEA
#COLORMEUNDERTHESEA #COLORMEUNDERTHESEA
#COLORMEUNDERTHESEA #COLORMEUNDERTHESEA
#COLORMEUNDERTHESEA #COLORMEUNDERTHESEA
#COLORMEUNDERTHESEA #COLORMEUNDERTHESEA
#COLORMEUNDERTHESEA #COLORMEUNDERTHESEA
#COLORMEUNDERTHESEA #COLORMEUNDERTHESEA
#COLORMEUNDERTHESEA #COLORMEUNDERTHESEA
#COLORMEUNDERTHESEA #COLORMEUNDERTHESEA
#COLORMEUNDERTHESEA #COLORMEUNDERTHESEA
#COLORMEUNDERTHESEA #COLORMEUNDERTHESEA
#COLORMEUNDERTHESEA #COLORMEUNDERTHESEA
#COLORMEUNDERTHESEA #COLORMEUNDERTHESEA
#COLORMEUNDERTHESEA #COLORMEUNDERTHESEA
#COLORMEUNDERTHESEA #COLORMEUNDERTHESEA
#COLORMEUNDERTHESEA #COLORMEUNDERTHESEA
#COLORMEUNDERTHESEA #COLORMEUNDERTHESEA
#COLORMEUNDERTHESEA #COLORMEUNDERTHESEA

#COLORMEUNDERTHESEA #COLORMEUNDERTHESEA
#COLORMEUNDERTHESEA #COLORMEUNDERTHESEA
#COLORMEUNDERTHESEA #COLORMEUNDERTHESEA
#COLORMEUNDERTHESEA #COLORMEUNDERTHESEA
#COLORMEUNDERTHESEA #COLORMEUNDERTHESEA
#COLORMEUNDERTHESEA #COLORMEUNDERTHESEA
#COLORMEUNDERTHESEA #COLORMEUNDERTHESEA
#COLORMEUNDERTHESEA #COLORMEUNDERTHESEA
#COLORMEUNDERTHESEA #COLORMEUNDERTHESEA
#COLORMEUNDERTHESEA #COLORMEUNDERTHESEA
#COLORMEUNDERTHESEA #COLORMEUNDERTHESEA
#COLORMEUNDERTHESEA #COLORMEUNDERTHESEA
#COLORMEUNDERTHESEA #COLORMEUNDERTHESEA
#COLORMEUNDERTHESEA #COLORMEUNDERTHESEA
#COLORMEUNDERTHESEA #COLORMEUNDERTHESEA
#COLORMEUNDERTHESEA #COLORMEUNDERTHESEA
#COLORMEUNDERTHESEA #COLORMEUNDERTHESEA
#COLORMEUNDERTHESEA #COLORMEUNDERTHESEA
#COLORMEUNDERTHESEA #COLORMEUNDERTHESEA
#COLORMEUNDERTHESEA #COLORMEUNDERTHESEA
#COLORMEUNDERTHESEA #COLORMEUNDERTHESEA
#COLORMEUNDERTHESEA #COLORMEUNDERTHESEA
#COLORMEUNDERTHESEA #COLORMEUNDERTHESEA

#COLORMEUNDERTHESEA #COLORMEUNDERTHESEA
#COLORMEUNDERTHESEA #COLORMEUNDERTHESEA
#COLORMEUNDERTHESEA #COLORMEUNDERTHESEA
#COLORMEUNDERTHESEA #COLORMEUNDERTHESEA
#COLORMEUNDERTHESEA #COLORMEUNDERTHESEA
#COLORMEUNDERTHESEA #COLORMEUNDERTHESEA
#COLORMEUNDERTHESEA #COLORMEUNDERTHESEA
#COLORMEUNDERTHESEA #COLORMEUNDERTHESEA
#COLORMEUNDERTHESEA #COLORMEUNDERTHESEA
#COLORMEUNDERTHESEA #COLORMEUNDERTHESEA
#COLORMEUNDERTHESEA #COLORMEUNDERTHESEA
#COLORMEUNDERTHESEA #COLORMEUNDERTHESEA
#COLORMEUNDERTHESEA #COLORMEUNDERTHESEA
#COLORMEUNDERTHESEA #COLORMEUNDERTHESEA
#COLORMEUNDERTHESEA #COLORMEUNDERTHESEA
#COLORMEUNDERTHESEA #COLORMEUNDERTHESEA
#COLORMEUNDERTHESEA #COLORMEUNDERTHESEA
#COLORMEUNDERTHESEA #COLORMEUNDERTHESEA
#COLORMEUNDERTHESEA #COLORMEUNDERTHESEA
#COLORMEUNDERTHESEA #COLORMEUNDERTHESEA
#COLORMEUNDERTHESEA #COLORMEUNDERTHESEA
#COLORMEUNDERTHESEA #COLORMEUNDERTHESEA
#COLORMEUNDERTHESEA #COLORMEUNDERTHESEA
#COLORMEUNDERTHESEA #COLORMEUNDERTHESEA

About
CIDER MILL PRESS BOOK PUBLISHERS

Good ideas ripen with time. From seed to harvest, Cider Mill Press brings fine reading, information, and entertainment together between the covers of its creatively crafted books. Our Cider Mill bears fruit twice a year, publishing a new crop of titles each spring and fall.

"Where Good Books Are Ready for Press"

501 Nelson Place
Nashville, Tennessee 37214

cidermillpress.com